To Connor

Kingfisher Books, Grisewood & Dempsey Ltd,
Elsley House, 24–30 Great Titchfield Street,
London W1P 7AD

First published in 1991 by Kingfisher Books

Text copyright © Jane Salt 1991
Illustrations copyright © Gerald Hawksley 1991
All rights reserved

BRITISH LIBRARY CATALOGUING IN PUBLICATION DATA
Salt, Jane
First words about my world.
1. English language. Words
I. Title II. Hawksley, Gerald
153.124
ISBN 0 86272 813 4

Cover design by Pinpoint Design Company
Edited by Karen Gray
Phototypeset by Southern Positives and Negatives (SPAN),
Lingfield, Surrey
Colour separations by Scantrans Pte Ltd, Singapore
Printed in Portugal

FIRST WORDS
ABOUT MY WORLD

Jane Salt
Illustrated by
Gerald Hawksley

Kingfisher Books

Introduction

Young children learning to talk love to try out their new words and sharing a book with you is an ideal way for them to do this. FIRST WORDS contains pictures of over 200 objects in familiar and amusing situations for you and your child to talk about together.

● Let your child decide how much time you spend talking about each page. He or she will want to return to favourite pages and sections again and again.

● Talk about each picture. Ask questions like 'What is the little girl doing?' or 'Can you think of a name for the little boy?'

● Relate the pictures to your child's own world by asking questions such as 'You've got some shoes like that, haven't you?'

● Encourage your child to tell his or her own story using the pictures.

● As your child gets older you can help his or her development as a reader and writer by drawing attention to the written words under the pictures.

● Most of all, have fun reading and talking about this book together!

Contents

Garden games	8
Down our street	34
Time for playgroup	50
A walk in the park	64
A visit to hospital	82
On the farm	92
Seaside holiday	110
In the wildlife park	130
At the supermarket	146
It's a parade!	166
Back home	184
Word list	186

Garden games

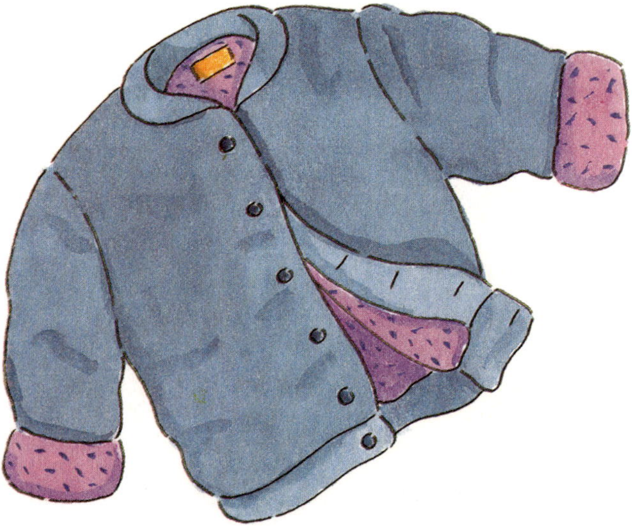

jacket

trainers

rabbit

hutch

tree

leaves

branch

caterpillar

bird

nest

eggs

thrush

sparrow

starling

bird table

butterfly

ladybird

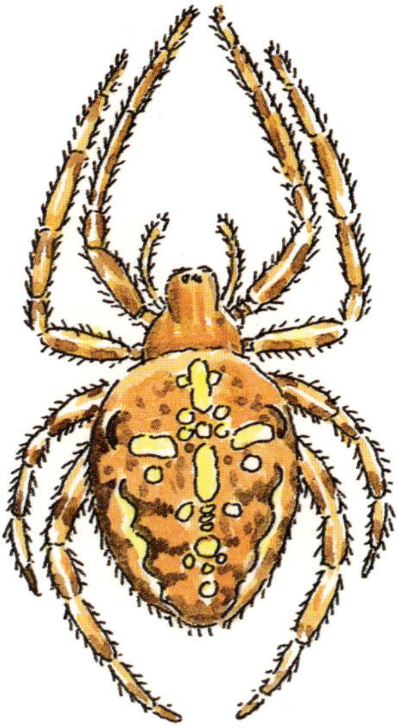

spider

snail

worm   soil

seeds

trowel

hose

flower

flower pots

rake

wheelbarrow

gate

swing

tricycle

cream

plasters

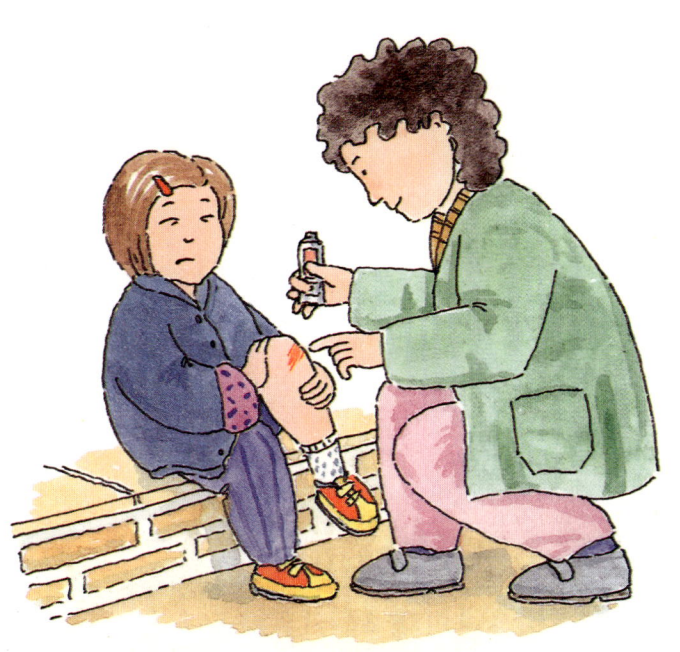

tent

picnic

Down our street

wellington boots

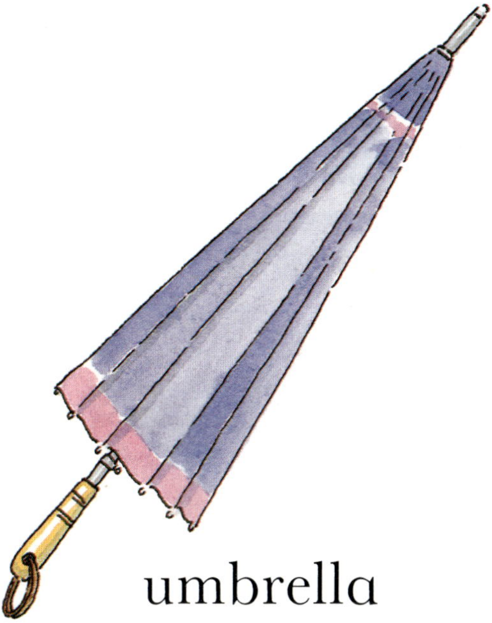

umbrella

stamp

Granny and Grandad
5 Main Street
Oldtown

letter

rainbow

bus

motorbike

fire engine

lorry

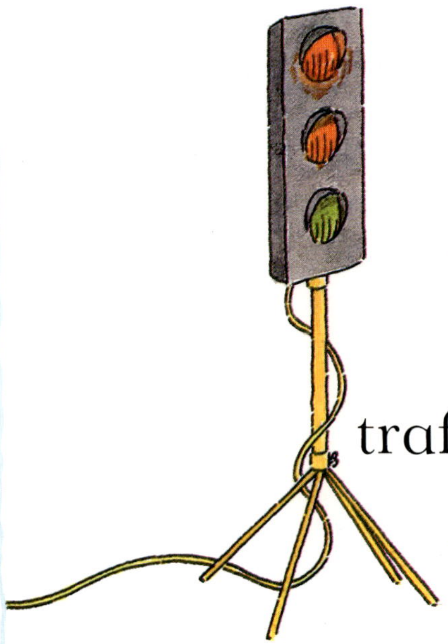

traffic lights

drill

cement mixer

digger

bulldozer

crane

Time for playgroup

Sarah

Kelvin

pegs

notice board

typewriter

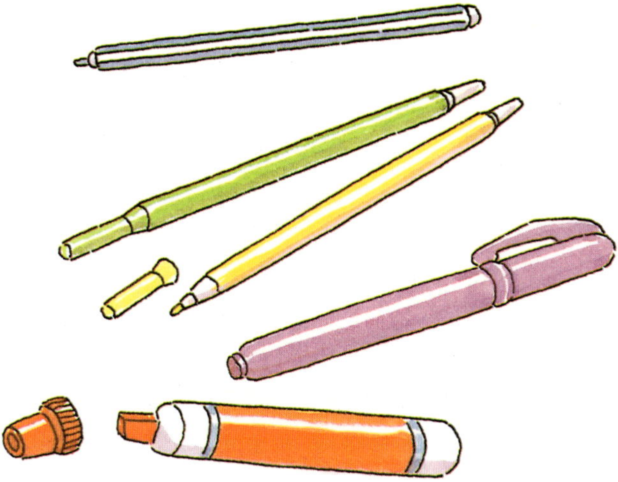

pens

fish tank

fish

helmet

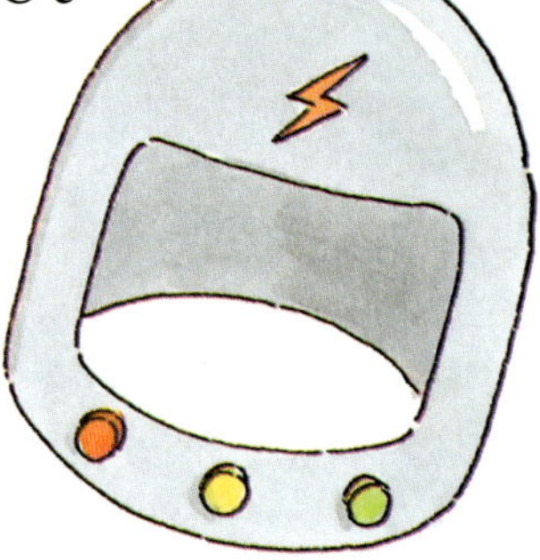

hat

cap

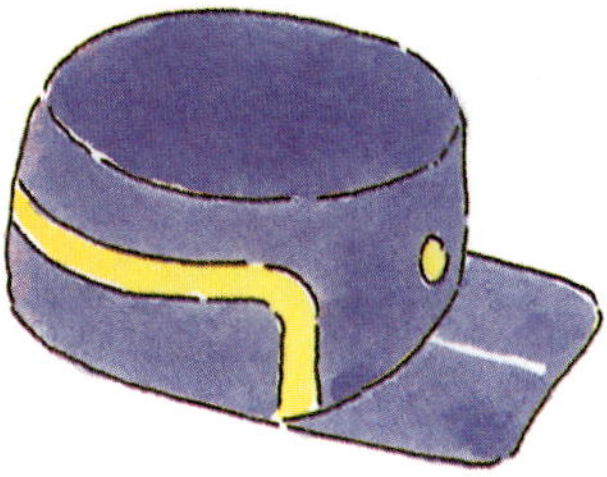

crown

guitar

tambourine

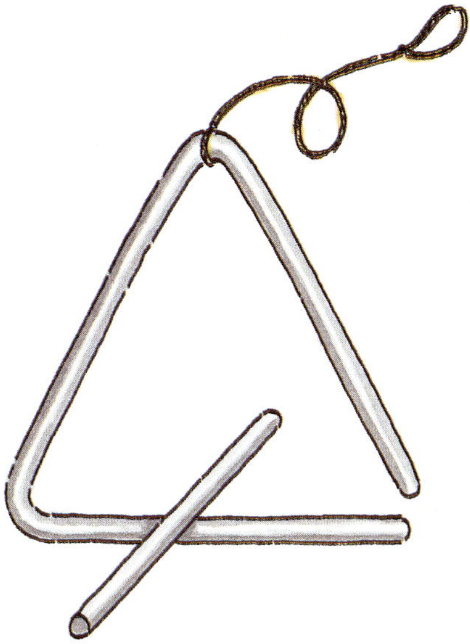

triangle

recorder

songbook

piano

dog

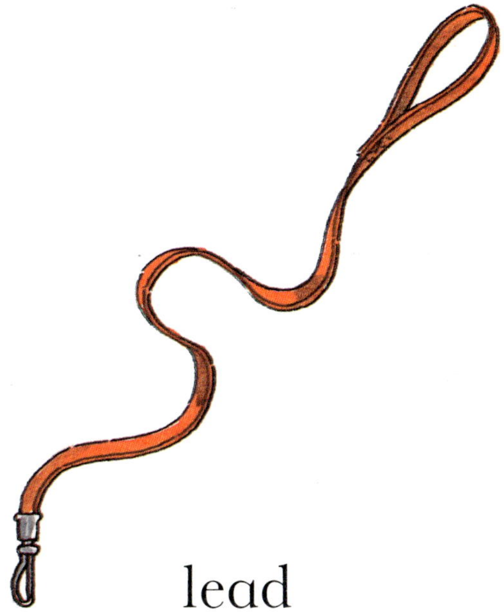

lead

rose

pansy

tulip

daffodil

climbing frame

slide

bench

see-saw

swan

duck

frog

pond

ice cream

litter bin

kite

roller skates

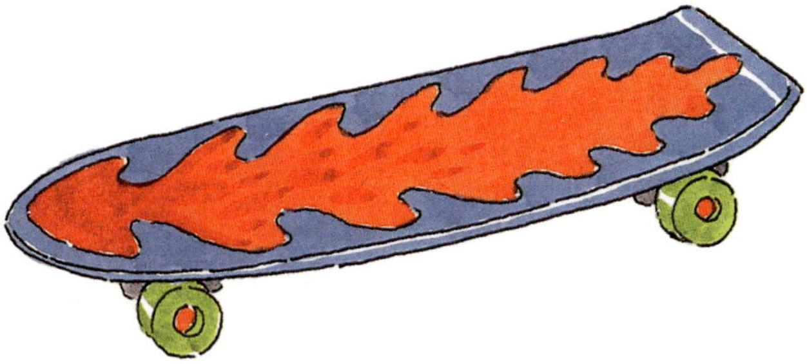

skateboard

bicycle

A visit to hospital

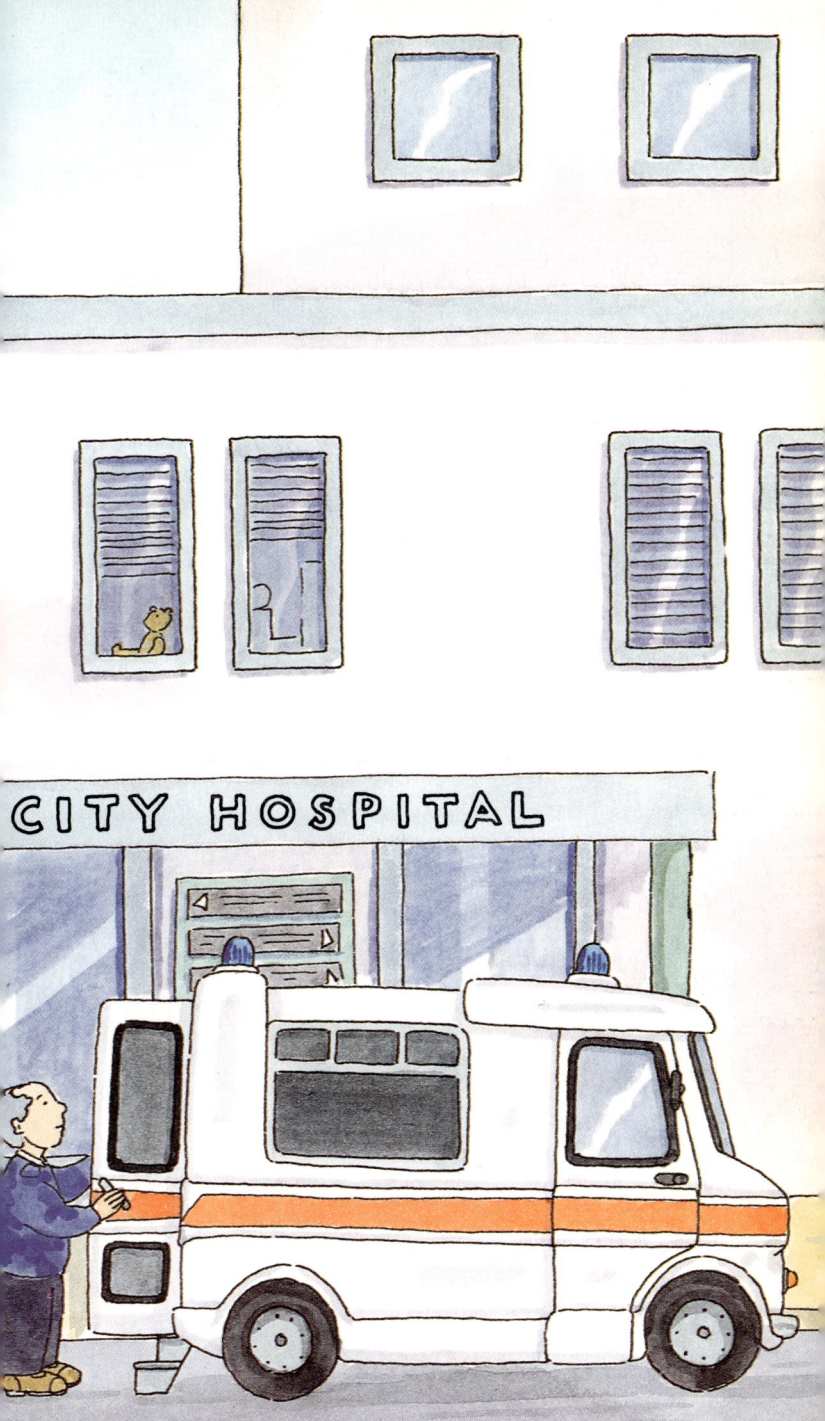

ambulance

doctor   nurse

thermometer

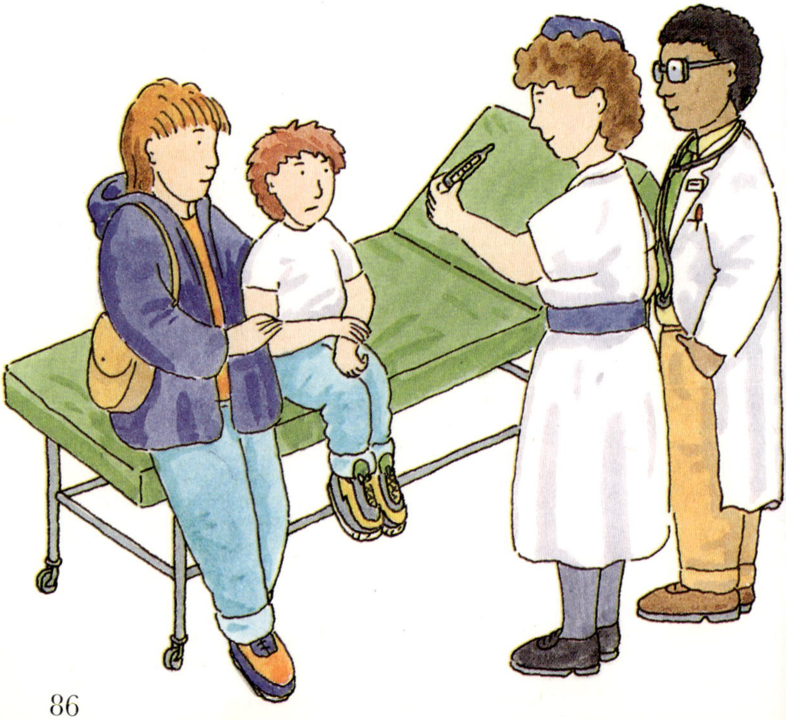

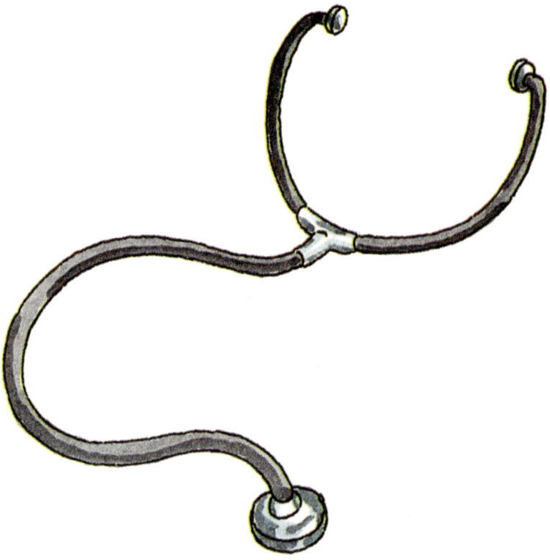

stethoscope

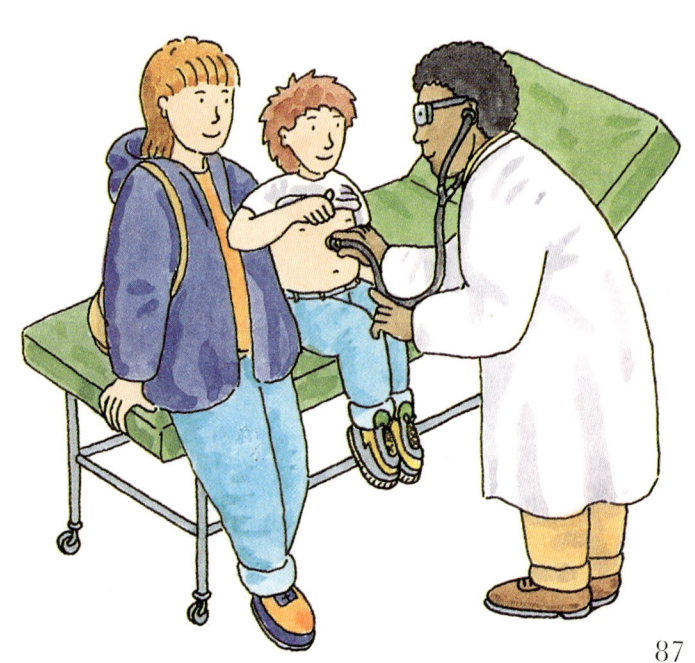

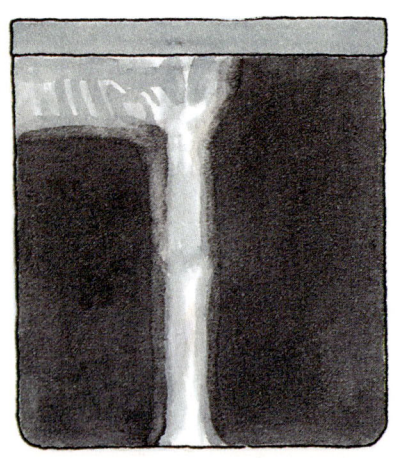

X-ray

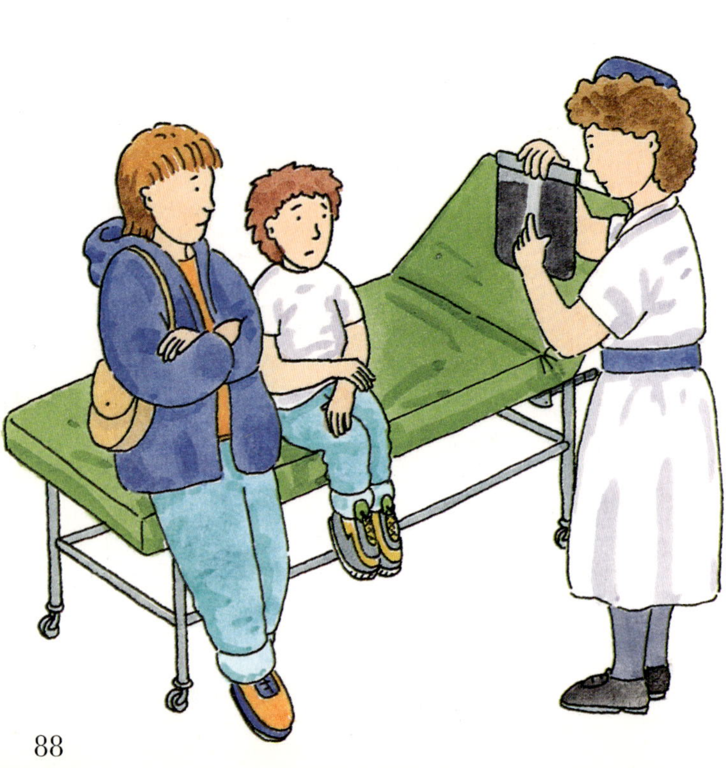

bandage

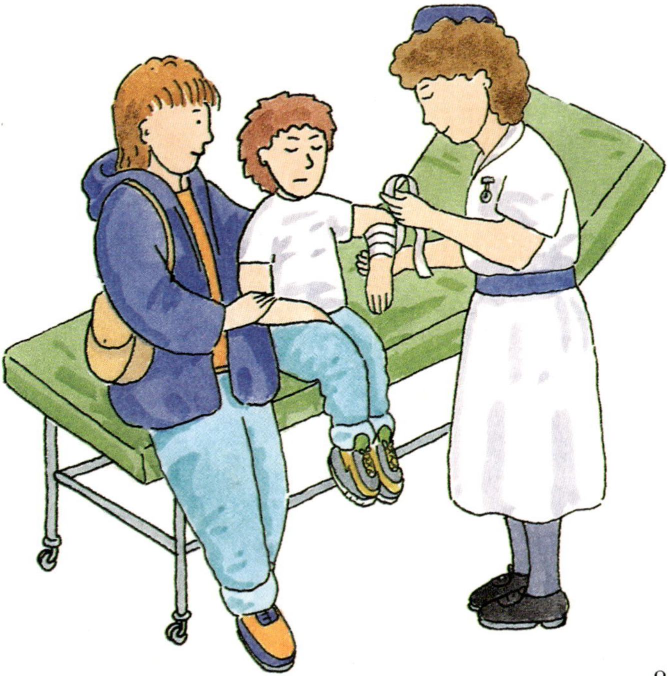

89

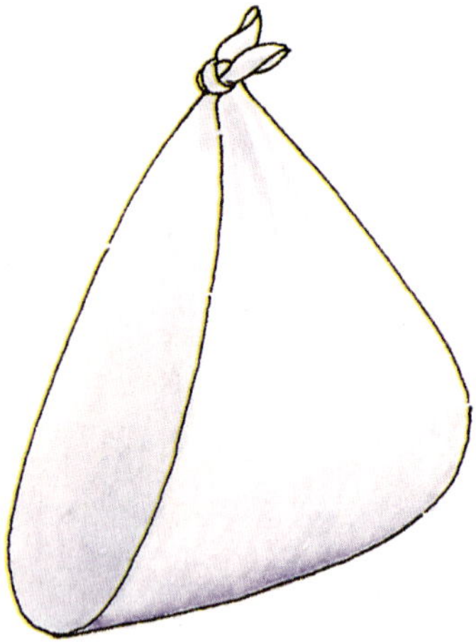

sling

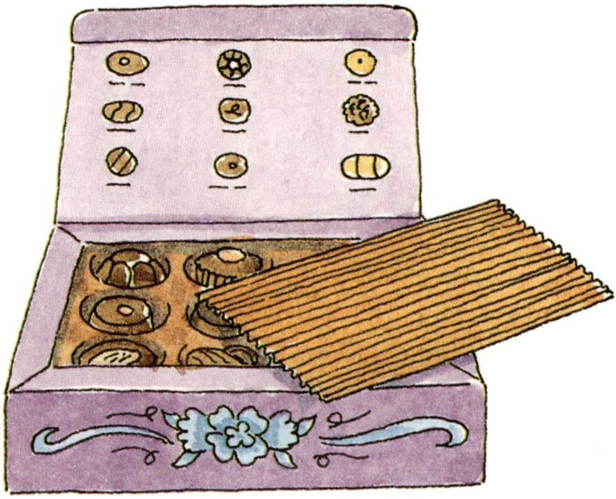

chocolates

hill

river

field

wood

owl

swallow

woodpecker

crow

fox

mouse

deer

squirrel

farm

farmhouse

barn

stable

horse

foal

sheep

lamb

pig

piglet

cow

calf

hen

chick

goose

gosling

goat

kid

tractor

Seaside holiday

sun

sand

sea

beach

swimming costume

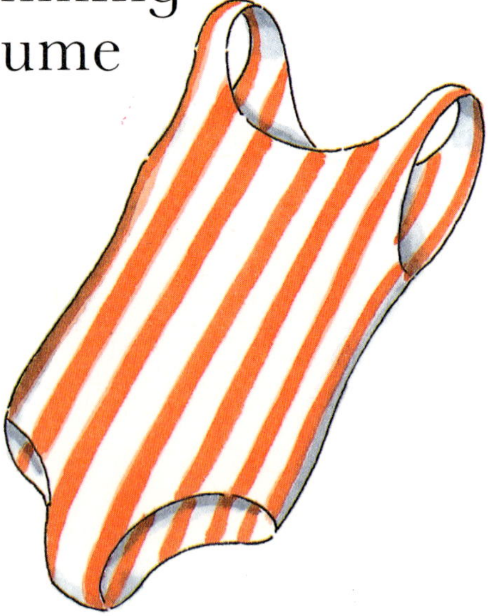

sun hat

sunglasses

parasol

deck chair

spade

bucket

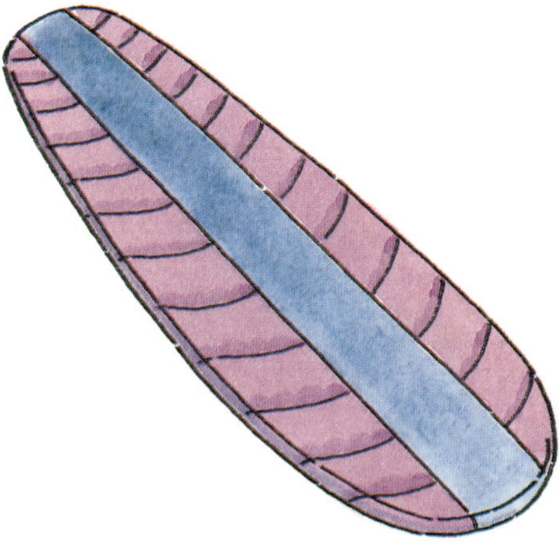

surfboard

beach ball

shells

crab

seaweed

rock pool

flippers

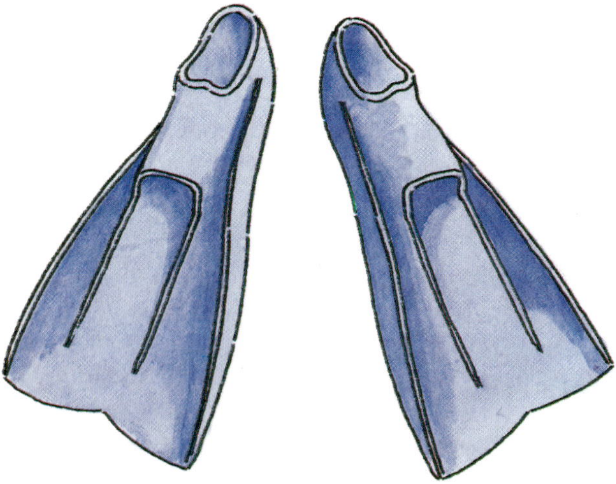

goggles

snorkel

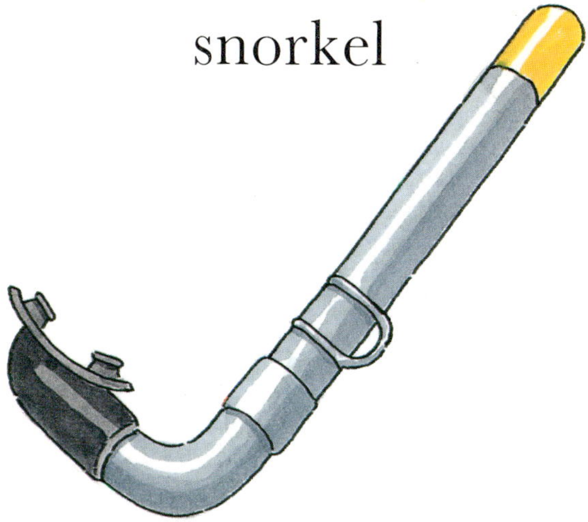

dinghy

ship

yacht

rowing boat

seagull

camera

gorilla

chimpanzee

orang-utan

giraffe

camel

rhinoceros

hippopotamus

bear

panda

koala

kangaroo

parrot

ostrich

flamingo

tiger

zebra

lion

cheetah

elephant

turtle

penguin

crocodile

snake

walrus

seal

At the supermarket

WONDER SUPERMARKET
Welcome!

entrance

shopping list

trolley

basket

can

box

packet

bottle

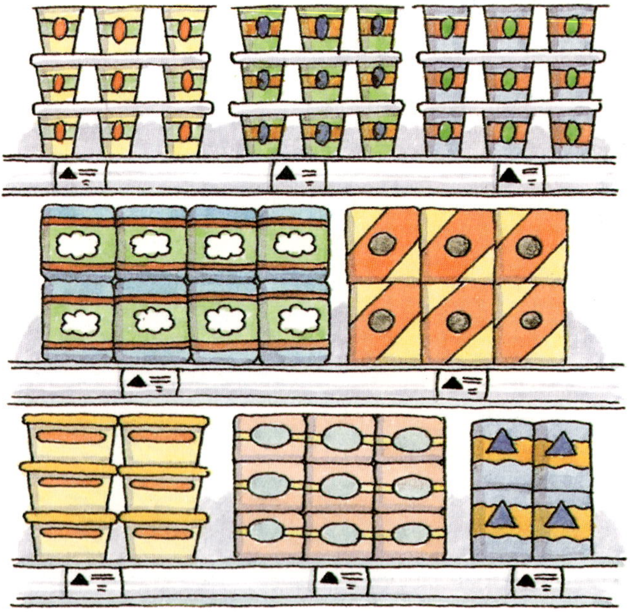

shelves

freezer

book

plant

till

wallet

money

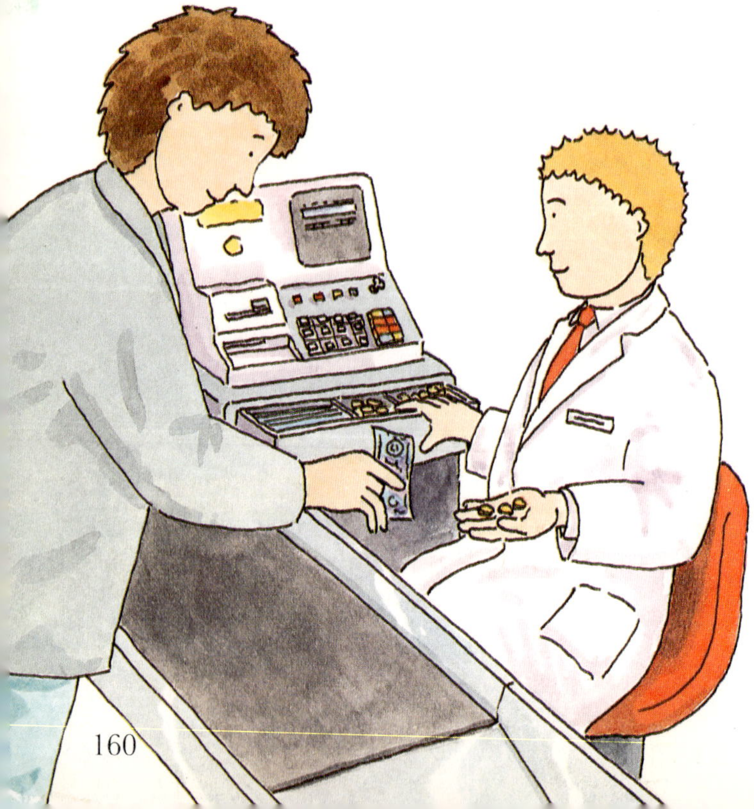

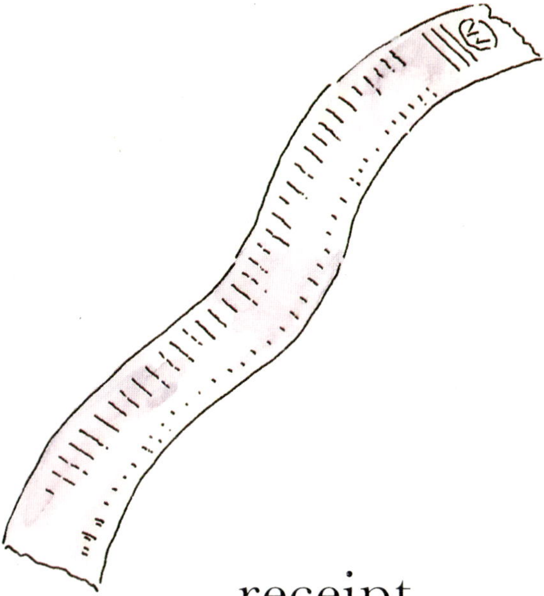

receipt

WONDER SUPERMARKET
Thank you for your custom

exit

car

keys

car seat

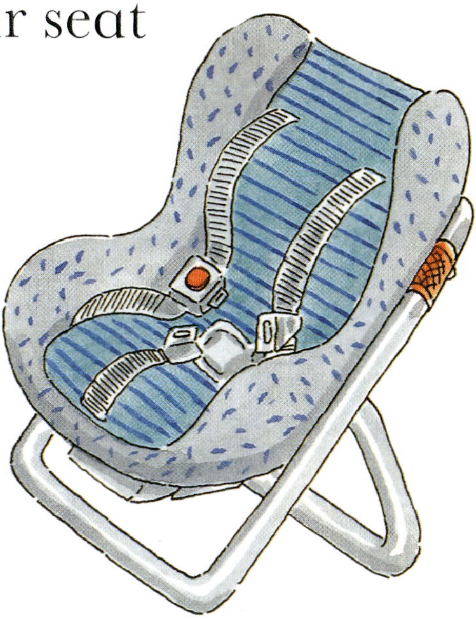

It's a parade!

balloons

streamers

drum

trumpet

saxaphone

cymbals

clown

juggler

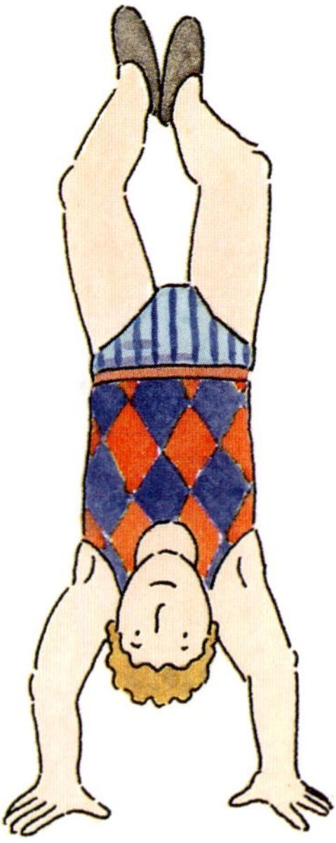

acrobat

stilt walker

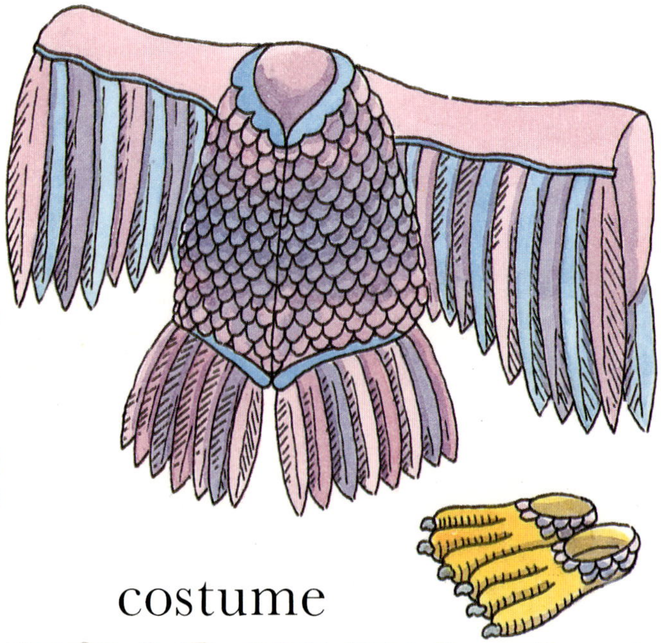

costume

masks

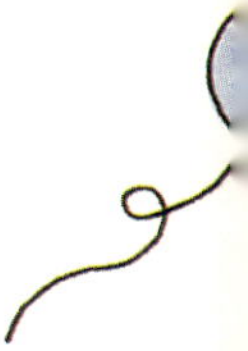

dragon

moon

fireworks

Back home

Word list

A
acrobat 176
ambulance 84

B
balloons 168
bandage 89
barn 101
basket 151
beach 113
beach ball 121
bear 136
bench 72
bicycle 81
bird 16
bird table 19
book 156
bottle 153
box 152
branch 14
bucket 119
bulldozer 48
bus 40
butterfly 20

C
calf 105
camel 134
camera 129
can 152
cap 59
car 163
car seat 165
caterpillar 15
cement mixer 46
cheetah 141
chick 106
chimpanzee 132
chocolates 91
climbing frame 70
clown 174
costume 178
cow 105
crab 122
crane 49
cream 31
crocodile 144
crow 97
crown 59
cymbals 172

D
daffodil 69
deck chair 117
deer 99
digger 47
dinghy 126
doctor 85
dog 66
dragon 180
drill 45
drum 170
duck 74

E
eggs   17
elephant   142
entrance   148
exit   162

F
farm   100
farmhouse   100
field   95
fire engine   42
fireworks   183
fish   57
fish tank   56
flamingo   139
flippers   124
flower   25
flower pots   25
foal   102
fox   98
freezer   155
frog   75

G
gate   28
giraffe   134
goat   108
goggles   124
goose   107
gorilla   132
gosling   107
guitar   60

H
hat   58
helmet   58
hen   106
hill   94
hippopotamus   135
horse   102
hose   24
hutch   13

I
ice cream   76

J
jacket   10
juggler   175

K
kangaroo   137
keys   164
kid   108
kite   78
koala   137

L
ladybird   20
lamb   103
lead   67
leaves   14
lion   141
letter   38
litter bin   77
lorry   43

M
masks   179
money   160
moon   182

motorbike 41
mouse 98

N
nest 16
notice board 53
nurse 85

O
orang-utan 133
ostrich 138
owl 96

P
packet 153
panda 136
pansy 68
parasol 116
parrot 138
pegs 52
pens 55
penguin 143
piano 63
picnic 33
pig 104
piglet 104
plant 157
plasters 31
pond 75

R
rabbit 12
rainbow 39
rake 26
receipt 161

recorder 61
rhinoceros 135
river 94
rock pool 123
roller skates 79
rose 68
rowing boat 127

S
sand 112
saxaphone 172
sea 113
seagull 128
seal 145
seaweed 123
seeds 22
see-saw 73
sheep 103
shells 122
shelves 154
ship 126
shopping list 149
skateboard 80
slide 71
sling 90
snail 21
snake 144
snorkel 125
soil 22
songbook 62
spade 118
sparrow 18
spider 21
squirrel 99
stable 101

stamp 38
starling 19
stethoscope 87
stilt walker 177
streamers 169
sun 112
sunglasses 115
sun hat 114
surfboard 120
swallow 96
swan 74
swimming costume 114
swing 29

T

tambourine 60
tent 32
thermometer 86
thrush 18
tiger 140
till 158
tractor 109
traffic lights 44
trainers 11
tree 14
triangle 61
tricycle 30
trolley 150
trowel 23
trumpet 171
turtle 142
tulip 69
typewriter 54

U

umbrella 37

W

wallet 159
walrus 145
wellington boots 36
wheelbarrow 27
wood 95
woodpecker 97
worm 22

X

x-ray 88

Y

yacht 127

Z

zebra 140